MotherFlux
Erica Gillingham
Jem Henderson
JP Seabright

Published by Nine Pens
2024
www.ninepens.co.uk
All rights reserved: no part of this book may be reproduced without the publisher's permission.
The rights of the authors Erica Gillingham, Jem Henderson, JP Seabright to be identified as the authors of this work has been asserted by them in accordance with the Copyright, Designs and Patents act 1988.

ISBN: 978-1-917150-02-6
NS 010

MotherFlux is the collaborative work of three queer parent-poets from the margins of (m)otherhood.

From embryonic dreamers and pregnancy-performers to sleep-deprived newbies and seasoned second-timers, their poems are raw, messy, and unflinching reflections on what it means to be a parent, and to make a family. The pamphlet considers gender, sexuality, politics, and the body as it moves between heightened individual experiences to outright rejections of societal expectations.

These are voices recording in real time, mothering in flux.

Contents

 9 some possible parent names
10 Pregnancy Test
11 childbirth / shipwreck
12 your baby is the size of a grain of rice
14 I can't feel you but
15 maternity dress
16 maternity wear, but make it tomboy femme
17 Breast is Best
18 milk stuck
19 Tongue Tied
21 which one is the mother
23 performing pregnancy
24 mending a constellation of bruises
25 This is a miscarriage
26 Babyproof
27 "I want to be in that hug"
28 Nazi bra sized
29 *Mummy, you're a boy*
30 girls' play
32 in retrospect
33 Collecting Categories into Which I do not Fit
35 taxonomies
37 my existential crises were different before
38 Passport Control
39 salt
40 Pancakes
41 transparent

For Rufus, Lyra, Arthur & Rory

some possible parent names

with thanks to Jon Kinsman

// tomboy-momboy / bruised fruit / theytriarch / milf-whip / nurse bee / one trick pony / haversack / trolley dolly / peach mobile / pantomime horse / mamacita / come to daddy / separation anxiety / lactose intolerant / swap / once in a blue moon / tiny dancer / pop goes the weasel / queen elizabeth / mother theresa / papa smurf / baba / starship enterprise / the motherlode / a cold night in hell / seraphim / mothertongued / sticky back plastic / repair shop / tinned peaches / cara mia / someone i speak to only on religious holidays / sad beige / hello barbie / designated driver / twinkle twinkle / homecoming queen / rainbow warrior / papa lazaru / bab's cabs / face not recognised / oh i do declare / project 2025 / fascist state / gay panic / hot apple pie / daughter of the fifth house / motherfucker / polyglut / this is your last warning / enruptured / angel delight / end of the phone / trans mam / using up the leftovers / hubba bubba / what's the time mr wolf / chaotic neutral / oooooh nurse / alexander and the terrible horrible no good very bad day / glow in the dark / mama stardust / corpse locked in a cursed tomb / cow parsley / puppet maker / free mom hugs at pride / bit of ow's yer father / captain picard / clever quiz team name but they always come last / black betty / schrödinger's (mad) cat (lady) / i'm loving angels instead / popeye / undertaker to the hive / fuck buddy / i'll give you something to cry about / telekinesis / time for teletubbies / here's mud in your eye / chainsaw enema / see you later alligator / dysmorphic diva / preggers plays pop / feeling delicate / finger and thumb / cozzie livs / peewhit / london fox / motherflux //

Pregnancy Test

I attempt to inject some romance
as I insert the syringe inside you
press the plunger to splurge a
stranger's sperm into your vagina

my left hand holding onto yours
squeezed tight in concentration
eyes misty with emotional intensity
this moment of conception

but it doesn't work that first time
or the next repeated performance
with fixed smiles and crossed fingers
and several injections of hormones

a few missed months of tears and stress
some extra and expensive tests
you get pregnant on the fourth attempt
I'm not even there to make pretend

that I'm the one impregnating you
with this dollop of donated goo
it's almost emasculating
the irrelevance of my presence

I feel I've failed the first test
with so many more to come
all those times when I am less than
just a spare pair of hands

to wipe bottoms and wash bottles
neither mother nor father
but both and something other
I will not take it for granted

childbirth / shipwreck

'So many died in childbirth, she observed.
And so few in shipwreck' - After Sappho

if
I, in
another
century past,
would've died
in the act of birth
bled out / wrung out
a pint of blood only five
contained within the frame
that grew & grew to hold a child
of average size / a mother who had
wanted that baby so goddamn much
to be out of her body / yes / out of there
how then to reconcile the almost-death
with possible un-birth / the taste of salt
with no figure pulled from the water
endless unequivocal depths with
the fever pitch of waves
a tide already set
receding

your baby is the size of a grain of rice

your second baby is easier, they say
you've already been through this
the nausea, the first fluttering kick
half remember the water birth
the silence cut with first cry
the gristle of the umbilical cord

but i have forgotten it all
afterbirth, mastitis,
eight years of no sleep,
nappies, ABCs, nursing,
nursery, robot noises, lego,
hospital visits

i've forgotten the rules
obviously no beer, no cigs
but no soft cheese, no sushi?
no pâté, no vitamin a
(even though i've taken
my cod liver oil
daily since i found out -
it's just a week, is that okay?)

i remember the grasp of a tiny fist
pulling at my hair, fiddling
with the teething necklace
the flirty grab of a bum cheek
the only intimacy for weeks

cosleeping, separate beds
arguments, separation,
new city, primary school
new friends, new lovers
new papa this time round

i've forgotten the terror
exhausted, lying awake
stressing about maternity leave,
stretch marks, my swelling body,
the cost of living, the cost of dying,
worrying that writing poems
about miscarriage
have jinxed me
into having
a real one

I can't feel you but

the lavender has never smelled more amazing. I've stopped checking the loo roll for signs of spotting. I don't have much of an appetite, until I do, mixed with waves of nausea—and I am six again in a tent, awake, beside my father, also awake, scared, needing to pee, worried I'm going to be sick, really just frightened of the noises outside, my father tells me to take deep breaths to think to myself 'I'm not going to throw up. I'm not going to throw up.' until I fall asleep—& then I'm standing upright with one hand on the chipped laminate countertop & breathe packing my bag, grabbing my keys, leaving the house with you.

maternity dress

bought second hand because the second time i know the expense isn't worth it. my belly isn't showing, just the bloat around a baby the app says is the size of a plum.

my boyfriend calls me pretty when i come down the stairs i try not to recoil even though i'm not and i don't want to be - the dress a lie that sits between us saying G I R L.

I could have bought some jeans or chinos but i remember last time - having to ask for assistance to take them off once my belly popped, lying helpless on my back - a tortoise stuck under a relentless sun.

maternity wear, but make it tomboy femme

no animal print or chintzy florals or stupid sailor stripes
no pastel pink or constant black or every shade of beige
        I want ombre looks and button-up shirts
the softest plaids in technicolour
capsule wardrobes with mouth-watering names
girlfriend jeans with the deepest of pockets
strong, extra-long muscle tanks, fitted tees
cotton t-shirt dresses with cuffed sleeves
carefully curated trainer collections for widening feet
with coordinated pop socks, a whole range
coupled with a coupon for your next undercut
endless wool and summer shackets with hip allowance
expanding crew neck sweatshirts, sturdy enough to last,
built to be passed on to someone else like

Breast is Best

    You are crying   end of the world   sobs of despair
how could we do this to you?   mamma is away
    for a few days   the other one   is looking after you
this one smells different   murmurs angular words
    with an uncertain mouth   unable to pacify
        you with milk

    I try everything   rocking singing standing up
play wave music   whale moans   offer my baby finger
    and ciuccio   even the bottle   but you spit it out
none have the warm   suck of breast   the
        comfort of mum

    After hours of this   exhausted in my own despair
I offer a tit   I've seen it done   I know the angle   the latch
    the catch of the baby-shaped rugby ball   I massage my breasts
as if mining   a lost seam of milk   willing sap to rise
        to the occasion

    I present myself   this unprepared inappropriate body
that never expected   or longed for this   push dysmorphia aside
    sacrifice my flesh   proffering propitiation to this
        tiny angry god

    You grasp nipple greedily   then spit me out
you have been tricked   and rage at this injustice with
        night-splitting cries

    I am bone dry   an unprepared husk a body devoid of milk
a land with no sustenance   I am not your mother
    merely a spare parent   useless and unnecessary
all I can offer is love   but sometimes that
        is not enough

milk stuck

I am crying   quietly   a tear running
down my cheek   landing on baby head
mastitis her hand round my throat   my tit
running red vine fingers   across my chest

my husband offers to get formula   says
it's fine   *if you want to stop*
it's not a failing   honestly   i think it is
I will do everything to be mother   to be
a *real* mother   one who gets down

on the floor wipes snotty noses   grazed
knees   play dates   buckets and spades
but it starts here   on this rumpled sofa
this immolation me to you your tongue tie

knotting restricting milk   backwash
into red raised abscess   later aspirated
the nurse holding   the biggest needle
nine times mastitis visits   nine times

i seduce her   promising you i can be
something I was never given   while i hold
a hitachi magic wand   to my aching breast

Tongue Tied

Piena come un uovo
    your roundness containing
a new world within
    one I dare not penetrate
for fear I might crack the shell
    break the spell we have created

Our bilingual baby
    vocal yet inarticulate
my tongue tied as I hold her
    arms down to stop her moving
mamma held back in fear
    don't look now as the
lingual frenulum is cut
    for there is blood and tears
like Abraham sacrificing Isaac
    without the moral pat from god

Ankyloglossia gone
    we shake with outrage
at what we have done
    the consultant reassures
that all will be well
    my wife offers her breast
to this untethered mouth
    blood mingles with milk
she sucks and I feel sick
    with fear of how I could do
such a thing to my child

Piena come un uovo
    my heart is full like an egg
as her tongue tries words
    from two mother lands
crying her way into a world
    that little understands
how we three make a family
    our tongues let loose with love

which one is the mother

coat on
coat on, coat on
and boots, yes, your boots
yes, put your boots on
that's it

      into the buggy, go on,
      climb into the buggy
      green! yes, it's green
      yes, green and white
      it's time to go, my sweet
      we need to go

            no, your bus stays at home
            i know you love your bus
            yellow school bus
            yes, yellow school bus stays home
            baby go outside, yes, outside

                  day-day, day-day, day-day
                  no, you don't need your day-day
                  no, you're ok, no, you're ok
                  fine, here is your day-day
                  we need to go

      yes, mama go to bookshop
      mummy go to hospital
      baby go to childcare

yes, that is a sun
blue sky, grey sky
airplane

    high five, high five
    car! blue car! auntie blue car!
    yes, just like aunties'
    dog dog, hello dog dog, hello
    morning, hello, how are ya
    car! car!
    red car!

ee-i-ee-i-oooooo
A-B-C-D-L-M-N-O-P
next time won't you
s-ng with me
car! car! almost there
here we are, here we are
    knock knock, *baby do it*
            bye bye baby, bye bye

performing pregnancy

i rub my belly while i wait in line
ease this ache of pregnant
the tight tension of ligaments
caged around a baby yet to be born

my body belongs to everyone
as older ladies outstretch rub
the younger ones ask first
hands held aloft

my body is a Bernini statue
the rape of proserpina
marble squeezed under hands
hard and soft

my belly is too big for my jeans
i am dressed like a little girl
in dungarees and smocks

i am naked a lot in this heat
    in heat

ready again for his rough touch
building two new bodies
mine and theirs

mending a constellation of bruises

each morning

a new bruise
    alternate parts
thighs, stomach
    pin pricks bloom
into supernovas

in the mirror
    black cotton pants
metal tube of arnica
    cold, gently applied
to each injection site

the constellation
    marking the body
weeks into pregnancy
    risk and possibility
each new star burns

their lives
now shorter
than the one
who is
growing

This is a miscarriage

of justice of family promises of hereditary
expectations of cultural preferences of hand-me-down
baby clothes of midnight reassurances of unwanted advice
of potential babysitters of risotto al radicchio of much-needed
comfort of patronising looks of emergency phone calls of sharing
anecdotes of cancerous cells of mother-in-law jokes of deathbed promises
of shared experiences of la bella figura of human connection of childhood
memories of faded photographs of meningioma of brodo e pastina of La Festa della
Mamma of mothering of motherhood of grandmothers of Nonna Valeria of home of family of love

Thus, a blessing —
       I wish for you —
              grandmothers

Babyproof

it's summer and we're shifting furniture
sweating up and down the stairs in preparation.
the trees leafy green, growing fat with apples, plums.

inside, we've decided no cot this time,
just a moses basket and a bedside crib which i'm sure
won't get used like last time. a place to store pillows

instead of baby. a changing table makes sense, no need
for streams of wee to blight the new king sized mattress
i bought in acknowledgment that cosleeping is happening.

the dresser full of new babygrows, washed, and old ones
lovingly arranged in piles of yellow, green and white.
the sun comes through the window, consecrating the pavement,

our nest. outside, a fledgling magpie shrieks at his mother
pecks her for food, hopping and skipping. i picture grasping
fingers, pinching and pulling while baby takes milk.

"I want to be in that hug"

my daughter cries from the toilet seat now she can sit on her own with her big girl pants on as my wife and I take a rare opportunity to hold on to each other like storm-tossed ships in the night to briefly touch each other to acknowledge each other's tired battered-down hatch of a body to remember who we were to each other and rediscover who we've become and after wiping herself and washing her hands she runs to join us and we sweep her up into one fierce animal bundle holding on tight as we sway unsteadily in the lounge together hoping that she never forgets how loved she is in a world where this is in short supply and how lucky we are to live in a country where our family is legally allowed to exist and when she tells everyone with pride in her voice when picking her up from nursery "I've got two mummies!" that she always retains this sense of self-worth in who she is and where she comes from 'cause we can't help worrying that she'll suffer for this from our choice to bring a child into a world that is self-bent on destruction and hate when all we can do is love each other the more for it and hold on tightly while we can

Nazi bra sized

a dad at the school gates -
neck tattooed with eighty eight
it *could* be the year he was born -
we're all about that age, but I
stood a few more steps away
looked around when he looked my way

and now my tits betray me. 30HH
the label says. totalitarian titties
brownshirt knockers. fleshy faschy bosoms
which I can barely hold up, my back a wreck
and most men can no longer
look me in the eye

Mummy, you're a boy

my daughter declares with confidence
No I'm not, I reply
with some lack of certainty
Girls can have short hair too, I say
the word girl sticking in my throat
like her pink plastic chicco.

She pauses, gives this some thought
Mummy, you're a girlboy
I shrug, we accept this as truth.

~

I always imagined I'd make a good dad
play with my kid
encourage them in everything they do
tell them I love them
just like my own father
didn't.

I shrug, accept my truth as girlboy mumdad.
Sometimes, we make our own role models.

girls' play

how come grown ups don't get to play dress up? i don't remember the last time i got to wear a princess dress.

> // in their canonical texts of game studies, both Huizinga and Caillois relegate dress-up dismissively to the sphere of girls' play.

i put on a dress. i feel like a fraud - except now i'm pregnant. now i'm playing at being a lady & i'm good at it.

> // play (verb): engage in activity for enjoyment and recreation rather than a serious or practical purpose. "the children were playing by a pool".

maternity leave & i'm watching all my favourite cartoons while the baby in my belly presses into my pelvis. the sky is full of hot air & the rain is staying away & the kids play in the sprinklers & school is back in session & the temperature is rising. it's two days past my due date & i wanna fill up the birth pool with ice & rubber duckies, wallow

> // the most common playground-related cause of childhood A&E visits is falling from the equipment to the ground. children fall because they slip, lose their grip

or because they're children playing on monkey bars, swings, slides, merry-go-rounds & see-saws.

i'm slipping, falling - losing myself in the overdue heatwave no water death death death anxiety space where everything feels like labour or like braxton hicks or like the end of now & the beginning of something too holy.

that virgin whore thing has it all wrong. the most divine & feminine i'll ever feel is nine months pregnant being fucked by a man who whispers his devout little prayers to god.

> // rough-and-tumble play is when children do things like climb over each other, wrestle, roll around & even pretend to fight.

i'm not fighting with the medical staff, not insisting on my pronouns. is there anything more woman than being a mother? i'm here playing dress up, not trying to be me.

there's blood on the pad, blood on her glove. stretch and sweep - a sacrament. she touched my baby's head. they're coming any day now.

in retrospect

there are plenty of other things
I've done for one week:

circumnavigated a desert island in sturdy boots
pulled scoops in an ice cream shop, got fired
worn my grandfather's leather jacket as a prop
slept under a duvet covered in rose petals
flew 3,000 miles for a party I didn't even like
salt-baked on a sailboat, fantasied about a caravan
cried when a lover left us with only a note
scanned thousands of profiles for a sperm donor
painted every room in a house millennial pink
bought packs & packs of pregnancy tests
burned candles, broke wishbones, made altars
transported all the ones we never met

Collecting Categories into Which I do not Fit

Mother

>I am the other mother
>the unnatural one
>the one against nature
>
>I have a child
>she is my responsibility
>it says so on a piece of paper
>recognised in my home country
>   (for now)
>but not all
>
>Her other mother's country
>her real mother
>the proper one
>her birth mother's homeland
>does not recognise my role
>There's no space on their paper for me
>
>This unexpected child of mine
>is both terrible and miraculous
>and I am waiting to find out
>what I should do about this

Wife

>What is this word and
>what does it mean
>I've never felt it should apply to me
>only to another
>someone I have wrapped
>a ring around
>Someone to whom
>I have betrothed
>but not to me

How could I possibly
be someone's wife
I would be the perfect
house husband
Is this an option?

Woman

Too much man
in not enough woman
Too much male
in not enough female

Human

Exempt Human Specimen
This is the label
they have given me
I stick it on
without question

taxonomies

neigh neighs: horses, zebras, unicorns; also, seahorses
sometimes: giraffe, gazelle, donkey, and alpaca
occasionally, by mistake: cows ('moo moos')

ar-too: airplanes, elephants

nanas: bananas, the childminder's assistant, crescent moons

balls: full moons, planets, bubbles, balloons, all balls
sometimes: 'ball ball'

mine: mama's phone, found on a surface, held out to mama demanding to be taken, wants to help

'nack: anything that isn't fruit or vegetable or cheese or vaguely like any food you'd have for breakfast/lunch/dinner you know which cupboard they are kept in, like to share

bees: flies, ants, bugs, and, well, bees

bugs: ladybugs

berry: with an exclamation or a smile, raspberries are your favourite but strawberries, blackberries, blueberries also count.
delighted: you see strawberries everywhere

bus: all the buses, all of them, red bus, school bus, double decker bus, volkswagen peace bus, antique bus, appa bus, cece bus *also, at night or first thing in the morning*: I love you too

mama: your mummy and mama
    also: any person, animal, or object that is the larger of two, the smaller of which is 'baby'
    adj. something belonging to mummy or mama
    for two weeks, after my mom visits: mommy and mama
    mostly, now: mama and mama, two mamas

baby: you, baby, it was always you

my existential crises were different before

a sign that you are

      teething, hungry
      cold, disgruntled
      ill, or will be, soon

we lie awake   for hours

knowing at some moment
      after / before
we will / you would not
      exist / alongside

Passport Control

Italian far-right government limits parental rights of same-sex couples
    Al controllo passaporti
      dice l'ufficiale
 è registrata?

My wife looks at him
      then at me carrying our daughter
and says *no, non è possibile*
 It is not possible to meet
      the requirements of Italian law
  to document all children born
whether in the motherland
   or abroad and allow
       my half-Italian daughter
not only a passport
    but to officially *exist*

  The government have declared that without
a mother and a father
   the forms are null and void

       but there is no father for our child
   sperm and egg do not make
a parent   people make parents
    e l'amore lo rende possibile

salt

of the earth, the sea
bleeding, seeping, sinking
failing to feed you from my flesh
floor under knees, holding you tender
to my chest, naptime, bedtime, at your crib
two in the morning, the waves of ways you catch me
crab, octopus, oyster of my eye; we can go anywhere, my sweet,
across the bed, the flat, on to pavements, buses, cinemas
where once i strolled & breathed & waited
all the years & hands beyond this now
where dancing laughter sings
& i would know
the salt of you

Pancakes

We are making pancakes in September
- we missed it on Shrove Tuesday

you were still too small at Easter
- and not interested in cooking

now you want to help with everything
- standing on your special steps

so you can reach the kitchen surfaces
- and help me beat the mixture

I crack the eggs into a jug
- aware of memorializing this moment

imagining future scenes of mother and child
- making pancakes together

I aspire to this yet feel brittle as eggshells
- discarded in the bin

for you are young and full of life
- with everything ahead of you

and I –
- and I am not

you want to recover the shells remake the eggs
- put them back into their box

My daughter I am sorry the world is broken
- and I do not know how to fix it

transparent

it's february 22nd, 2023. I'm at my 12 week scan. baby is wriggling, waving tiny arms & showing tiny bum. my partner's face awed.

it's december 28th, 2022. my tongue hurts right on the tip. I google it - a folate deficiency but it takes two days for me to work out what's happening & to take a pregnancy test. It's 10pm & the two lines appear straight away. my partner's face dumbfounded.

it's july 12th, 2023 & the nurse says he when talking about the baby at the scan but I'm not sure if I didn't say it first because I've only been pregnant with a boy before & though it's eight years since, it's a habit.

it's january 25th, 2023. i'm at my booking appointment for my second baby, the list of questions neverending. weight. height. BMI. *is your partner supportive?* at no point do they ask my pronouns. *are you a boy or a girl?* feels redundant when I'm gestating a human. i'm told by the press it's offensive to scores of mothers insistent that only *shes* can give birth.

it's november 10th now, there's a circulatory system walking through the kitchen... no wait, that's Dr Manhattan. it's january 5th, 2023 & there's a circulatory system in my uterus.

it's august 28th, 2023. i'm 38 weeks & 5, same time that my firstborn came. there's no sign of baby. i break open two spiky green shells & reveal white & brown conkers. they're not ready yet.

it's april 20th, 2023. we announce i'm pregnant on social media. *it's a... baby!* i cringe at the thought of announcing the gender of someone who isn't here & hasn't made their mind up yet. it's just the same as shrieking *they've got a cock/pussy!* in the high street.

it's september 14th, 2023. baby bleeds onto my nursing top after a heel prick test. my milk has come in & my blood pressure drops dramatically causing me to shake uncontrollably. inept circulatory system.

it's january 6th, 2023, i am writing my birth plan, copy & pasting from my eight year old birth plan. it's july 26th, 2015. I am writing my birth plan. it is july 26th, 2023 & i am writing my pronouns onto my birth plan.

it's every day of my pregnancy. *doesn't she look great? isn't she carrying well?* the birth buddy app talks about he or she when talking about the baby. my seven year old is asked if he wants a brother or sister but he says he just wants a sibling.

it's july 12th, 2023. my 32 week scan shows that I can have a homebirth. I book the birthing pool & get asked my pronouns for the first time in my pregnancy.

it's august 23rd, 2023. my grandad Barry passes away after 15 weeks in hospital. the phrase one in, one out plays on a loop in my head while the baby does the jitterbug inside me.

it's september 9th, 2023. 2.46am. after only a 2.5 hour labour at home, I squeeze one last time & push out my baby girl into the birthing pool.

Acknowledgements

MotherFlux was written by Jem Henderson, Erica Gillingham and JP Seabright.

Jem wrote: *your baby is the size of a grain of rice, maternity dress, milk stuck, performing pregnancy, Babyproof, Nazi bra sized, girls' play, transparent*

transparent includes a reference to Alan Moore's *Watchmen*

Erica wrote: *childbirth / shipwreck; I can't feel you but; maternity wear, but make it tomboy femme; which one is the mother; mending a constellation of bruises; in retrospect; taxonomies; my existential crises were different before; salt*

JP wrote: *Pregnancy Test, Breast is Best, Tongue Tied, This is a miscarriage, "I want to be in that hug", Mummy, you're a boy, Collecting Categories into Which I do not Fit, Passport Control, Pancakes*

Passport Control contains text from the newspaper article *Italian far-right government limits parental rights of same-sex couples* by Colleen Barry, Associated Press (March 2023)

some possible parent names was written by Jem, Erica and JP and is dedicated to Jon Kinsman

About the authors

Jem Henderson (they/them) is a genderqueer poet from Leeds, winner of a Creative Future award for underrepresented writers. genderfux, their first collaboration came out February 2022. an othered mother, their first pamphlet, is out now from Nine Pens and a collaborative collection with Chris Cambell, small plates, is available from Broken Sleep.

Erica Gillingham (she/her) is a queer poet, writer, and bookseller living in London via Siskiyou County, California. She works as a bookseller at Gay's The Word bookshop and serves as the Poetry Editor for *The Signal House Edition*. Her debut poetry pamphlet *The Human Body is a Hive* was published by Verve Poetry Press, and her poetry and essays have been published in various journals, anthologies, and radio, including in *100 Queer Poems*; *365 Poems for Life*; *Queer Life, Queer Love*; and on BBC Radio 4's Short Cuts. She exists online at www.ericagillingham.com and @ericareadsqueer.

JP Seabright (she/they) is a queer disabled writer living in London. They have four solo pamphlets published and two collaborations, encompassing poetry, prose and experimental work. They explore themes of gender, sexuality, trauma and the climate crisis in their work, and have been nominated for a Pushcart Prize, Best of the Net, and Forward Prize (twice) as well as shortlisted (twice) for a Saboteur Award for Best Collaborative Work. More info at https://jpseabright.com via Twitter @errormessage and @jpseabright everywhere else.

www.ingramcontent.com/pod-product-compliance
Lightning Source LLC
Chambersburg PA
CBHW020133130526
44590CB00040B/609